YouTube Decoded

By
Marc Guberti

Your Free Gift

As a way of thanking you for your purchase, I am offering you a free ticket to the Content Marketing Success Summit.

The Content Marketing Success Summit showcases an ever growing list of speakers who will teach you how to create, promote, and optimize your content—and use that content to generate a full-time income.

If you are interested in achieving a full-time income from your content brand, then I recommend getting your free ticket for the **Content Marketing Success Summit** which contains the insights that will allow you to reach the next level.

contentmarketingsuccesssummit.com

Table Of Contents

Introduction

YouTube is the top social network to place your videos and grow your business. It's no wonder so many creators upload their content to YouTube. In any given minute, there's over 500 hours of video getting uploaded to YouTube. YouTube also has over 1 billion users ever since its humble beginning on April 23, 2005, when the first video was uploaded to YouTube.

With so much popularity, some believe the platform has become oversaturated and success isn't possible for the new creator on the block. That's just not true, and the data and examples prove it.

It's still possible to take your channel from 0 to 100,000 subscribers in a year. Is it hard? Oh yes, but there are people who do it to this day. While that's more of an exception than the rule, seeing some YouTubers achieve these results shows the platform is still filled with opportunity for new and seasoned creators alike.

I understand how frustrating it can be to grow a YouTube channel. Before I became consistent on YouTube, I was on and off with the platform. If you don't know how to leverage the platform, growth will be slow and the money won't be there.

In this book, I will help you grow your channel and start making money from your YouTube videos. It's possible for any creator to make a big splash on YouTube. The question boils down to how much work you want to put in to make it happen.

If you are ready to make the big splash on YouTube and massively expand your brand, keep reading.

Part 1
Setting The Foundation

There's no doubt that YouTube is one of the top social networks on the web, but how can we set ourselves for success on this platform? To kick things off, we are going to set the foundation for your YouTube success.

Choosing Your Channel Topic

Your channel should focus on something you're passionate about and can create videos about for a very long time. In my case, I'm very passionate about helping people make money with their content, and I can create videos on that topic for a lifetime.

You might be passionate about different things, but start with a channel topic on one of your passions that also has heavy demand. For instance, I am also passionate about running, and while I do see myself creating a channel around that passion in the future, it wasn't something I prioritized at the beginning of my YouTube career. A channel around digital marketing presents me with more opportunities than a running channel based on my current business and demand for topics within both of those areas.

Focusing on one channel and growing that audience first will give you a smoother growth trajectory for future channels you may decide to create. So if you have multiple passions you can make money with, understand that if you pick one but not the other now, you can create a second, third, or even more channels once your first channel gains momentum. One notable fact is that if you wait a while to start the second channel and focus on your main channel, it won't take as much time or work to grow future channels as it will take to grow your first channel.

What To Expect On YouTube
When you commit to creating and growing your YouTube channel, you will have to invest some time on the platform for you to expand your reach. In my experience, it takes around 2-3 hours each week for me to create videos but more time with the marketing.

When you reach the point of YouTube's search and organic traffic taking over, you have the option to dial back your manual marketing efforts and still gain subscribers and views. However, I don't recommend doing that as the more you promote your videos and bring people to YouTube, the more YouTube will reward you.

It's important to focus on a topic you're passionate about because there are going to be some days where you don't get any new subscribers. These days are especially common for most YouTubers when they first start their channels. If you focus too much on the subscriber number but not enough on how much you love creating videos and serving your community, you will not make it on YouTube.

Create great videos, show the love to your community, and get out there and market your videos…and the results will follow.

Video Equipment Set-Up

4

This is the step of the YouTube process that can greatly enhance the quality of your videos, but it can also hold back a ton of new YouTubers from taking action. I'll share my video equipment set-up shortly, but I want to address new YouTubers first.

When you are first starting out, it's more important for you to create videos and do what you love than it is for you to have the video equipment set-up and solid editing. Just create, create, and create some more.

My first videos were done just with my Mac Book Pro's built-in audio on an ironing board. The audio for these videos wasn't always great. If the computer got hot and the built-in fans turned on, the sound of the fans made it into the video's audio.

When I started recorded videos on my iPhone, the first few didn't have the same sound quality as my computer set-up (at that point, I had the mic, headphones, and all of those things for creating videos with my computer).

I focused on creating content first and then enhancing the experience as I continued along the journey and grew my audience.

A big mistake new YouTubers make is thinking they have to spend a ton of money on equipment and the right camera just to get started. Just use what you have and create great videos.

However, once you have created enough videos and have some traction on your channel, you may want to start thinking about your video equipment set-up. With that said, here are some of my recommendations...

- **Blue Yeti Microphone** — this is by far my favorite microphone to use. The sound quality is amazing and it only costs around $100. This microphone attaches to your computer.

- **Blue Yeti Pop Filter** — the pop filter removes most of the background noise and protects your microphone from saliva and moisture damage. Most people don't think about the saliva and moisture damage, and to be honest I surely didn't, but if you want to preserve your microphone and use the same one longer, get the pop filter.

- **Headphones** — I only use a set of Mpow Thor headphones because they were a Christmas gift. However, any set of headphones will do, even the very basic and common Apple headphones will get the job done. Don't invest heavily in headphones when most of the cheap options work.

- **Video Editing** — There are a variety of free options such as iMovie, but I prefer to use ScreenFlow because it would take forever for me to get anything done in iMovie. ScreenFlow (or Camtasia depending on which device you use). I personally have never used Camtasia but know that they are both very similar. They also allow you to record your screen, so if you prefer to deliver slides than be seen in your videos, these are both great options for you.

- **Lavalier Lapel Microphone** — This is the microphone I use for my iPhone. It only costs around $20 and is great if you want to create videos on your iPhone. You'll sound crisper and there will be less background noise. You can also hook this microphone up to your computer or tablet, but I only recommend it for the iPhone. With that said, if you are on a tight budget, it is a less expensive option compared to the Blue Yeti microphone.

You may also want to consider a stand for your smartphone to reduce shakiness in your video. And if you like to create videos on the go, an air vent phone mount will allow you to record hands free quality videos in your car. Air vent phone mounts are the same things Uber drivers use to keep their phones in front of them while they drive. For their purposes, they need the GPS. For your purposes, you can get a better, still angle for creating quality videos on your commute without holding and looking into your phone while driving (which I'd never encourage anyone to do).

Are there more expensive pieces of equipment that will enhance your audio quality? Definitely…but who's going to notice them.? There's a point where when the audio is good, you've got rapidly diminishing returns for enhancing that audio.

Just to quickly use some technical terms, 128 kbps is the bit rate of the sound equivalent of what you'd hear on the radio. You could then argue that a file with a bit rate of 1,280 kbps would sound better. Will it? Slightly. Will people notice? Probably not. You'll also make your file much bigger and uploading it will take forever. Most of my files are under 128 kbps because no one's going to notice the difference or think about it unless the sound quality is bad (i.e. too much background noise).

And if you find yourself on a service that has a monthly quota for gigabytes (i.e. Libsyn and other podcast hosting sites have a monthly GB quota, Vimeo, etc.), one file at 1,280 kbps would easily take up your entire allotment. Good luck producing a weekly podcast.

I don't care much for kbps in my videos and don't know my video's average kbps. It's not a metric you should think about.

I just listen to my videos before publishing them, and if the audio sound good to me, I know they'll sound good to the viewer. I'm just using this example to demonstrate that there isn't much of an incentive to improve your audio quality once you have the basic set-up in place we covered earlier. Producing quality videos and doing the marketing is far more important than slightly better audio.

Engaging With Your Community

One of the most rewarding parts of starting a YouTube channel is the community you'll develop over time. You can see how your content is impacting people and get feedback on what type of content to incorporate in future videos.

I love my YouTube community and every comment I get. You can get more people in your community to participate by asking people to comment on something specific within one of your videos. For example, if I'm comparing X and Y in one of my videos, I'll ask viewers to drop a comment and let me know if they like X or if they like Y.

Your YouTube community can also be a great hub for future YouTube video ideas. I often look at the comments and see what questions my viewers have. Those questions often turn into future videos.

One important thing to note is that as your channel grows, you will come across some trolls. You'll have to stay strong during these times and think more about your community that has supported you than one troll with one hateful comment.

And to be honest, trolls are actually good. They indicate you're doing something important, but there's a sneaky element to trolls and using them to your advantage. I'd ignore them in real life, but YouTube is a different story.

Right now, a big social proof indicator is the amount of comments your videos receives. More comments means more engagement which means YouTube will push out your video to more people.

When you reply to a comment, a video instantly goes from having just one comment to now having two comments. This helps the YouTube algorithm. You may want to consider feeding the trolls by replying to their comments. They'll reply back to you, and you can get into a deep conversation with trolls.

It is very important to think before you write these comments because some of these conversations can get heated. However, if you and a troll engage back and forth, you can get 10 or more comments on your video very quickly and YouTube will push it out even more.

This book contains strategies and tactics that won't require you to reply to trolls to boost your videos, but it does help if it's something you want to do. And if you do reply to trolls in this manner, you'll have a deeper appreciation for the community you've built and the people who leave positive comments on your videos. In my experience, you'll get far more positive comments on your videos than comments from trolls.

With that said, you want to focus more of your time on the people who love your content. These are the people who will watch each of your videos, hit the like button, and possibly become customers.

Experimenting On The Platform

YouTube is a platform in constant motion. While the core foundational pieces will remain the same, YouTube will continue making changes to their platform to attract more viewers and retain them for a longer period of time.

As a creator, you need to continue experimenting with the platform. Test different video styles and look at the analytics to get a clear picture of how well you are doing. YouTube is a science that requires experimentation for you to figure out what best works for your channel.

This book will give you a variety of strategies and tactics that will help create videos, make money with those videos, and reach more people. However, this book will just be the starting point of your experiment. If you decide to take YouTube seriously, I recommend watching other YouTubers in action and pay attention to what they're doing to create more engaging content, monetize that content, and get views.

Combine those strategies and tactics with your own YouTube strategy, and one of your experiments can pay off and result in a surge in your channel's growth. To build up on your YouTube strategy, we're going to take a deep dive into creating videos that make money and get exposure…right now.

Part 2

Creating Great Videos

What makes a great video? There are plenty of tactics to make great videos, but great videos have two things in common.

The first thing is that they provide value, but what exactly does that mean? We hear about providing value but rarely get an explanation.

When thinking of value, you have to focus on your audience. It's easy to come out with a new video, think it's valuable, but the analytics tell a different story. If people are running away from your video, or it has a massive drop in views compared to your other content, it's not valuable to your audience.

I am a very active runner and will likely run 100s of marathons in my lifetime. I've ran the mile in under 5 minutes. If I came out with a video detailing how to break five minutes in the mile, it would be valuable to an audience of runners.

However, that's not my core audience for my main channel. If I create a separate running channel that grows a community of runners, then that video becomes valuable to that community.

But the viewers on my main channel want to learn how to use digital marketing to grow their businesses. And when I see a specific video category take off, I create a ton of extra content around that topic.

When I saw that my videos about YouTube Marketing were getting significantly more views than my other content, I dialed down and the next few videos I published were about YouTube Marketing.

If a certain marketing topic doesn't do well, I stop creating videos around that topic because my audience has spoken. That's what value is. It's understanding what your audience wants and giving a comprehensive tutorial or experience that matches their expectations.

The second thing great videos have in common is superior editing. One of the things I talk about often is to become a YouTube viewer. Every week, I'm watching other people's YouTube videos, but I'm not always watching videos within my niche.

Each time I watch an engaging YouTube video, I think about how it engaged me and why I kept watching. For most videos, the editing makes a big difference because it creates pattern interrupts. Changes of scenery, some music that pops up in the middle of the video, and YouTubers moving from one part of the room to the other during cuts are some editing approaches that have kept me and others engaged.

Superior editing will increase your watch time, an essential staple for the YouTube algorithm that will determine how often they recommend your videos to their users.

With that said, one thing to not do is to just sit in your chair, talk for a few minutes, and not do any editing. Your content can be on point, but the editing gets people to stick around. We'll cover editing and how you can delegate it later.

Coming Up With Great Video Ideas

Great video ideas aren't always the creative ones. Sure, trick shot videos and others like those can get creative and be good ideas. Pick the right idea, create world class content around that idea, and you can go viral.

Going viral will obviously grow your audience and have a positive effect on your entire channel and how your videos show up on YouTube's algorithm.

However, I don't like a strategy that relies on going viral. Strategies that rely on going viral are just as reliable as you or me making a basket from the other side of the court while wearing blindfolds. Instead, I like a strategy that allows you to achieve sustainable growth and then build up on that momentum without wearing blindfolds.

So what is a great video idea? To put it simply, it's a video idea that worked well in the past and works well today. Ideally, it's a video idea in your space that is picking up momentum and is trendy in that moment.

I'll give you two examples of how this works. The first YouTuber we'll talk about is Jennelle Eliana. She fully embraced the van life and created a few videos detailing her van lifestyle. The videos are well edited and put Jennelle's amicable personality on full display. I watched two of her first three videos.

So did millions of other people. In fact, her channel grew to over 1.3 million subscribers within 3 weeks of its launch. It turns out the van lifestyle is a trendy topic right now and she capitalized on it. Jennelle also had a big Instagram following going into her channel, but not the kind of following that could typically result in 1.3 million subscribers for a new channel in 3 weeks.

This is an example of how going viral can help you. Jennelle didn't plan for it, but it happened anyway. It is a blindfolded full court shot that you can't count on for your YouTube strategy, but it feels great if you make it.

Now here's where things get interesting…

Jennelle's quick growth in a short period of time led to two things. The first thing that happened was a trove of conspiracy theory YouTube videos with people falsely alleging that she was getting help from YouTube or knew someone in the company. Those weren't the only conspiracy theories, but those were the main ones.

Besides, what else could explain her success…while also resulting in a clickbait video for the people who created those conspiracy videos? There are ethical ways to grow your YouTube channel, and then there's that, but there is a light at the end of this tunnel.

The second thing that happened was YouTube experts creating videos detailing how Jennelle went viral and different tactics you can use to grow your YouTube channel.

While going viral on YouTube is very hard to truly plan, growing on YouTube is much easier to plan and systematize. These videos were providing value while riding the hot trend.

So instead of the title "5 Ways To Grow Your YouTube Channel," people were using titles like "How Jennelle Eliana Grew Her You-Tube Channel To 1.3 Million Subscribers In 3 Weeks"

My YouTube mentor Anthony Ambriz created one of those tutorial videos a few days after Jennelle went viral. He called the video "Jennelle Eliana Van Tour How She Went Viral! | 1M Subscribers in 1 Month | Video Creator Secrets."

The title gives you an idea of what will be discussed in the video, but it also has popular keywords. At that time in particular, "Jennelle Eliana" became a popular keyword with few videos around that keyword.

Anthony ended up dominating the YouTube algorithm and becoming one of the first 3 results on Page 1 of Google for "Jennelle Eliana." He wasn't there anymore when I last checked, but even getting that coveted Google spot for a short period of time will still put you in front of a massive audience.

Just one more important stat before we move on…

At the time of writing, Anthony gets a few hundred views for each of his videos. The Jennelle Eliana video he created?

- Over 30,000 views right now
- Over 700 comments
- Over 800 likes
- 100s of extra subscribers within days of publishing that video

And that one video accounts for over 85% of his entire channel's views at the time of writing.

He could have called the video something like "How To Get 1 Million YouTube Subscribers In 1 Month" and focused on a different YouTuber. He could have published the Jennelle Eliana video months instead of days after her name became a heavily populated keyword.

Timing was key for that video's success. And that's what a great idea is. Something that's proven to work. Combine that with something trending and some marketing, and you can get a massive overnight boost for your YouTube channel. Yes, I did say overnight and that's not clickbait.

But opportunities like these don't come often. So what do we do in between? We can create videos around topics our audiences have engaged with in the past, but we can do something else...

Look at the most popular and recent videos from other creators and create very similar videos to those.

That's one of the "darker" secrets of YouTube. Take what's working for someone else and copy it. The only things different are your personality, some of the content, and that it's you instead of the other person in the video.

However, it's not as "dark" as it sounds. In fact, we all do it at some point. Don't think for a second that this is the only book you can find on YouTube. You're not in a unique business. If you're a photographer, there are other photographers out there. If you're a YouTuber in real estate, there's a bunch of other real estate YouTubers out there sharing the same stuff.

I'm currently subscribed to two real estate YouTubers (Graham Stephan and Meet Kevin). Many people who are subscribed to one are often subscribed to the other. And each one pays attention to what the other is posting.

Sometimes, you'll see a video published on one of their channels that gets popular. You'll probably then find the same video with a slightly different name and content published on the other's channel 1-2 weeks later. And there's no bad blood. In fact, they sometimes do collaborations and are good friends.

The big mistake creatives make is writing down a list of ideas that's solely based on which ideas come to mind first. There's no research involved to determine if the idea will actually rank on YouTube and get views.

Creating videos is fun, but doing that research when coming up with the ideas is the difference between YouTube just being your passion project and YouTube being a place that actually grows your business and makes you a full-time income.

My Two Favorite YouTube Keyword Research Tools

Finding trending keywords in your niche and popular videos from other YouTubers requires research on YouTube's platform.

However, research isn't just about finding what's working right now. It's also about finding the right keywords that will work over the long-term.

Two tools I like to use for my keyword researching purposes are vidIQ and Tube Buddy. vidIQ allows me to discover which key-words have high demand and low competition. Tube Buddy on the other hand is great for when I want to add tags to my videos. They'll give you more than enough tag suggestions to reach 500 characters (YouTube's maximum number of characters for all tags combined).

Knowing these tags then impacts my YouTube description because I'll organically put a bunch of them in the description.

Both of these keyword research tools are Google Chrome exten-sions, so you will have to use YouTube on the Chrome browser to get the full benefits of these resources.

Creating The Video Script

For some people, a video script will be their compass. Others pre-fer to go off-the-cuff because they're already experienced with de-livering video and audio content.

I'm going to share how to create a script, and regardless of how confident you feel about delivering quality content, I want you to create a script.

For a while, I resisted the idea of scripting my videos. I'm a seasoned podcast host who has done over 700 interviews if you include virtual summits. I've done thousands of videos as well, so I can take a topic off-the-cuff and make a great video out of it.

But the script isn't just for creating great videos. Scripts also help you with your marketing, getting people to watch more of your videos, and the editing. Even if you're not going to edit your videos, a video script will make it easier on your video editor to edit the video the way you want it edited. That will, in effect, make it easier on your wallet if you decide to delegate video editing.

Here's a simple video script rubric you should use for all of your videos...

Hook to grab attention	Something that grabs attention. A question, stat, or a busted myth will do	Audio, video shots, sound effects, etc.
Intro	Let people know who you are and briefly what your channel is about. Less is better, but make sure you invite people to subscribe if they aren't already. In this intro, briefly state something you do. I like to say in my intros that I am "the podcasting coach teaching people how to launch, grow, and monetize their podcasts." Right away I mention I'm a coach which makes converting viewers into clients much easier.	Audio, video shots, sound effects, etc.
Emphasize the video topic	Highlight a problem you're providing the solution to or, for a channel more on entertainment, what's about to happen in the video	Audio, video shots, sound effects, etc.

Key talking points	The main part of your video. Make sure you ask engagement questions to get more comments and ask for likes at some point. Work those engagement points into your script so you know when to ask for them and what to ask for. Also write down which of your past videos and other content you want to mention.	Audio, video shots, sound effects, etc.
Summary and Call-To-Action	Briefly summarize your video and give your subscribes a relevant call-to-action. For a content marketing video, I'll invite people to get their free ticket to the Content Marketing Success Summit. And I always invite people to subscribe to my channel...because it's never too late to subscribe to my channel.	Audio, video shots, sound effects, etc. Make sure you include an end-screen that invites people to subscribe to your channel.

When you plan out your videos in this manner, it's easier for you to create high quality videos that grow your channel and spread awareness for your other content.

Editing Your Videos To Increase Watch Time
Watch time, retention rate, and clickthrough rate are YouTube's three most important metrics. We'll talk about clickthrough rate

later, but the watch time and retention rate are both critical parts of the creation process.

The best way to thrive with these two metrics other than creating quality content is through quality editing. Video editing can turn a good video into a great one with multiple angles, audio effects, and other pattern interrupts.

There are plenty of tools available to edit your videos. Free ones like iMovie and Movie Maker give plenty of options. While Adobe Premiere Pro is a popular choice among YouTubers who have been at it for a while, I personally prefer to use ScreenFlow to edit my videos.

A general rule of thumb for editing videos is to have at least one pattern interrupt every minute. Anything from an audio effect to a different camera angle qualifies. Incorporating more of these pattern interrupts will make your videos more engaging.

If you prefer to delegate the video editing, I recommend finding someone on onlinejobs.ph, Fiverr, or UpWork to get the job done. You'll either have to pay video editors on a per video or per hour basis. If you produce many videos that require minimal editing, the per hour basis would be the better approach. If you want highly detailed editing for each of your videos, you should find a video editor who will charge you per video instead of per hour.

In either case, your video script will play a key role in speeding up your video editor's time. The video script doesn't just contain everything you want to say. It also contains all of the video edits you want to see in the video and when you want to see them. This will make it easier for you or the person you hire depending on which approach you take.

Without a video script like the one above, video editing can be extremely tedious. Video editing can still take a considerable amount of time even with the script, but you'll easily save at least 30 minutes with the script in place.

Create A Content Editorial Calendar

An editorial calendar will keep you on track to produce epic content. You can use this calendar to determine and maintain a consistent publishing schedule that aligns with your product launches.

YouTube is only a great social network if you approach it like a great content creator. A strategic editorial calendar will give you enough content for your viewers with enough room to ride on certain trends.

Ideal content editorial calendars are planned several months in advance, but leaving extra room for trends and capitalizing on them will make a big difference for your channel. Remember the trend towards content around Jennelle Eliana? You couldn't have planned for it in your content editorial calendar. That's why you should leave some space open for trends like those.

I drop multiple videos each week but always leave an open space for a trending video topic just in case. Leaving those open spaces also gives me more flexibility to create content around timely topics (i.e. if I'm launching a virtual summits, I can create videos around the topic of my virtual summit and promote the summit as a call-to-action).

Pro Tip For Podcasters

I know many people in my community are podcasters, and I am a big advocate for more people starting their own podcasts. It's an incredible opportunity for business owners to reach more customers that I talked about in another book called Podcast Domination.

That's why I included this part of the book for all of the podcasters out there.

The next time you interview someone for your podcast, make it a video interview. Turning your podcast episodes into video interviews gives you the content to upload to YouTube. You can then turn the video file into an audio file and use that for your podcast episode.

By the way, if you are new to podcasting, I recommend Libsyn as a great podcast hosting site, and you can use the coupon code Breakthrough to get the rest of this month and the following month for free.

But believe it or not, that's not the pro tip. The pro tip starts before the interview. Earlier I shared my two favorite tools for doing research on YouTube (vidIQ and Tube Buddy). With those tools, I'll search for keywords related to the interview and the guest's expertise before I interview that guest.

Then, I'll find a keyword that is performing well and turn that keyword into the question. I'll set up the question in such a way where the guest gives me a longer response than usual. Then, with some edits and commentary I add later, that becomes my video.

Here's an example of how this played out for a recent Profitable Public Speaking episode…

I interviewed my friend Jess Tiffany on how you can use LinkedIn to get on more stages. Going into the interview, I knew that would be the topic because it matches up with Jess' expertise.

After some research, I didn't see much traction for keyword phrases like "How to use LinkedIn to get speaking engagements" on YouTube.

After enough research, I found two good keywords…

"How to get clients with LinkedIn"
- vidIQ Search Volume: 30
- vidIQ Competition Score: 7

"LinkedIn Marketing"
- vidIQ Search Volume: 51
- vidIQ Competition Score: 14

Basically, those stats tell me there's a bunch of demand for those keywords but not enough videos to fill that demand.

And each word in that keyword is important. Change "how to get clients **with** LinkedIn" to "how to get clients **using** LinkedIn" and you've got a bad keyword with little traction.

I ended up calling the video this...

LinkedIn Marketing | How To Get Clients With LinkedIn Using These 3 LinkedIn Tips (w/Jess Tiffany)

Now that I identified popular keywords that make sense for the episode, I had to ask a question that would bring that keyword to life.

Most of the conversation was focused on using LinkedIn to get more speaking gigs because this was for the Profitable Public Speaking Podcast. However, I slipped in this question for the sake of creating an optimized YouTube video:

"What are your 3 top tips for getting clients with LinkedIn?"

Jess answered that question in about 5 minutes. After the interview, I added about 4 minutes of commentary and edited the video. The commentary is exclusive to the YouTube video which gives podcast listeners a reason to watch that video.

Before recording the interview with Jess, I told him in advance to be ready for the 3 tips question. I then gave him some time to write down what tips he would cover for that part of the episode.

In the video, I also mention that the rest of the interview can be found on the Profitable Public Speaking Podcast. I usually release the video before the episode, so I tease the podcast episode in that video and point people to the podcast.

So instead of just giving guests the podcast episode to promote, I'm also giving them a video to promote. The video is published at least a week before the episode which makes promoting both pieces of content doable for the guest.

I publish 3 podcast episodes each week which gives me up to 3 YouTube videos each week. This does not include any solo video(s) that I publish. The only challenge with this frequency is that you have to meaningfully promote all of those videos for that frequency to make sense.

If you publish 4 videos each week, one of them gets 100 views, but the other three get less than 10 views, that's going to have a negative impact on your channel's performance.

If you're in this situation, one thing you can do is put multiple guests in the same video. Let's say I was interviewing five people about LinkedIn during separate times. I then ask each of them for one of their top tips for getting clients with LinkedIn.

To avoid any redundancies, I'll tell each person pre-interview what tips have already been covered.

Then, when that video comes out, 5 LinkedIn experts are promoting it instead of just 1 LinkedIn expert. Not to mention that I'll be promoting the video too.

You can take this a step further by asking multiple questions that turn into videos and then releasing all of the videos over a span of weeks to give your viewers more content and drive more attention to your podcast.

Repurposing your content is one of the most important strategies you can utilize to become present on more platforms and grow your brand. Video interviews is one of the best ways to quickly create many smaller pieces of content.

Turning Your Videos Into Articles

Turning snippets from your podcast episodes into YouTube videos that are more than just start-to-finish interviews will work wonders for your video creation. However, video and podcasting are just the beginning of the frontier. While we'll focus more on what you can specifically do for videos, these tactics also apply if you host a podcast and want to use the strategy I mentioned earlier.

The spinoff content you should focus on first is articles. Each time you come out with a new video, you can embed that video into a blog post. Some people take the transcription of their video and turn that into the written component while others summarize the video and urge their readers to watch the video.

I prefer to summarize the video to entice people to keep watching because that will help with turning readers into YouTube subscribers. I will also follow suite on LinkedIn and Medium by essentially copying and pasting that article on those platforms.

When I write new content that's not repurposed from a YouTube video, I create content around videos I've recently released and embed as many of them in that blog post as possible. For instance, I wrote a LinkedIn article called 3 Proven Strategies To Rapidly Monetize Your Podcast.

Marc Gubertl posted this

3 Proven Strategies To Rapidly Monetize Your Podcast

Marc Gubert on LinkedIn
August 14, 2019

This topic was intentional since many of the new videos on my channel were geared towards podcasting at that time.

I looked at my video titles for inspiration on what the proven strategies to rapidly monetize your podcast would be.

After looking at my videos, here were the three strategies I came up with and the corresponding videos for each one…

Strategy #1: Get Sponsors — I embedded the videos "Get More Podcast Sponsors In 2019 And Beyond — Podcast Tutorial" and "Podcast Affiliate Marketing Strategy | Make Money Promoting Affiliate Products On Your Podcast."

Strategy #2: Get Clients From Your Podcast — I embedded the video "Podcast Monetization For Beginners | Getting Clients Fast."

Strategy #3: Organize A Virtual Summit Around Your Podcast
— I embedded the video "How To Monetize Your Podcast With Virtual Summits | Make Money With A Podcast."

One article had four video embeds. This is how you can use your YouTube channel to inspire new content and turn it into an article.

I can even go back to that article a few weeks later and make it a video that mentions those four videos I embedded in that article. So if you see a YouTube video on my channel called "3 Proven Strategies To Rapidly Monetize Your Podcast," you know how it happened.

Part 3

Monetizing Your Videos

Most people follow the create, then promote, then monetize model. The problem with that model is that you may start getting some traction, but you don't have any money to show for it. That's why we are going to discuss monetizing your videos before we get into the marketing.

There are plenty of ways to monetize your videos. The most well-known way to make money with your videos is to have Google Adsense in the background. Once you get 1,000 subscribers and your 4,000 hours of watch time within a 365 day period, you're allowed to use Google Adsense for your videos.

So you will have to continue hitting a consistent 4,000 hours of watch time each year. On the other hand, if you are at 1,000 subscribers but never gain or lose a subscriber again, you'll still be a YouTube Partner with the ability to run Adsense on your videos.

However, this isn't the way that most video creators make a full-time income on YouTube. It's a way some people make full-time incomes on YouTube, but these are usually the people who are getting millions of YouTube views each year. The amount you get paid per view depends on your niche, but you need over 1 million views each year to make something that could look like a full-time income on YouTube if you're only using Google Adsense (Note: most likely not above $50,000 for 1 million views with Adsense alone…so it depends on what full-time income means to you).

Sure enough, YouTubers still pursue the partnership status because Adsense is an easy way to make money from your videos. You set it up once in under a minute and your videos keep making you money. However small it may be in the beginning, those numbers can noticeably grow as your YouTube channel grows.

We already covered video editing as a great way to boost watch time, but live streaming is another great way to boost your watch time. We'll talk more about live streaming in the marketing portion of this book.

With Google Adsense out of the way, let's talk about ways anyone can make money on YouTube even if you aren't a partner yet. Spoiler alert: You'll earn a lot more with these upcoming strategies than with Google Adsense alone.

Promote Your Products In The Video
If you have a book or training course related to the video at hand, promote that product during the video. You'll make far more money promoting your own products than you'll make from Google Adsense.

With Google Adsense, you make around $2-$3 for every 1,000 views you get. That's 1,000 views. If even two of those people buy your $3 Kindle book, you'll make more money selling two Kindle books than you would from those 1,000 views.

Now what if 10 of those 1,000 viewers buy your $3 Kindle book? That's definitely more money than Google Adsense.

And now, what if 3 of your 1,000 views buy your $97 course? All of a sudden, we're talking around $300 per 1,000 views instead of the $2-$3 per 1,000 views that Google Adsense would give you. This is how smaller channels make it on YouTube…and it's also something bigger channels do to reap bigger profits.

Instead of focusing exclusively on growth, full-time YouTubers focus on monetization. This is how some YouTube channels with fewer than 1,000 subscribers bring in more revenue than YouTube channels with over 10,000 subscribers. It's all about what you're promoting in your videos.

How you promote your product and how often you promote your product depend on the length of your video. You should first promote your product a few minutes into the video because the majority of your viewers will still be viewing your video at that point.

And when I say promote your product, I'm not talking about an all-out webinar style sales pitch. If you hit on a topic related to your training course, mention the training course and talk about it for 5-15 seconds. While talking about it, show your viewer what the training course looks like and some of the lessons they'll learn. You can do something similar for books and services.

If you can subtly mention your product or service without turning your video into a sales pitch every few minutes, that would be ideal. You can also promote your product again on your video's end screen to drive more attention to it.

If you have all three types of offerings, I recommend promoting your books when they come out but mainly focus on the training courses. People on YouTube are comfortable with binging good video content, and that's the exact thing a quality training course allows them to do. You can later sell your services in your funnel, something we will also be talking about soon.

"But I Don't Have A Product Yet"

We've all been there…and you may be there right now. You hear about people selling their books, training courses, and services, but you don't have one of those yet. You have a few options for getting your product out quickly…

#1: Become a coach and tell people they can hire you — There's very little work you have to do on the front end to set this up. Just use software like Acuity to create your calendar and allow people to schedule a time for free strategy sessions and coaching sessions.

#2: Prelaunch a book or training course — You can create pre-order campaigns and promote those in your YouTube videos. Who says you have to have the product finished before you can start making sales?

#3: Affiliate marketing — This will make sense for most people. In fact, even though I have many products in the marketplace, I'm still promoting products as an affiliate. If you find products in your niche that are converting well, you can promote them in your videos. You can even do the occasional product review if it makes sense for your channel.

Those are the different options you have for promoting products on your channel even if you don't have a product quite yet. The first two are pretty self-explanatory. For affiliate marketing, the only beginner challenge is finding products that you would want to promote as an affiliate.

To kick things off, Amazon has millions of products to choose from. Their 4% commissions aren't ideal based on the types of affiliate commissions you could be getting from other products, but a 4% commission is better than no commission. And if the person who buys your affiliate link decides to buy other products too, those product sales are also credited to your account.

Some people who initially went through one of my Amazon affiliate links to buy a book ended up buying cameras, scooters, and other expensive items that I don't promote with my Amazon affiliate links. I'd never turn down a commission on those items, but there are affiliate offers with higher commissions available.

The ideal way to find affiliate offers is to do a Google search for brands and topics you love. If you love a certain makeup line and post makeup related tutorials, look up the brand on Google and put "affiliate program" at the end of that brand's name. Do this with enough products and you'll start to build up an arsenal of affiliate programs and links as you sign up for those affiliate programs.

You can also use resources like Clickbank, CJ Affiliate, JVZoo, and LinkShare to find additional affiliate products to promote on your channel.

Make sure you have the links to all of the products you promote in your videos towards the top of your description. You want to optimize the description with the keyword first, but 1-3 paragraphs later should be where all of your links reside.

Get Viewers On Your Email List
YouTube and every other social network helps business owners get more attention. However, an algorithm change can easily divert that attention elsewhere and leave you back at square one. While earlier algorithm changes were more drastic and necessary to prevent YouTubers from gaming the system, algorithm changes can still happen.

That's why you should never rely on social networks like YouTube for preserving your audience. These social networks are great for discoverability and cultivating an audience, but you don't own that audience.

The only way to truly own an audience is to have those people on your email list. That way, you get full control over how often you communicate with your audience and know that they'll actually see your email in their inbox.

Plus, turning your viewers into email subscribers is an excellent way to monetize your YouTube channel. That's because when you get your viewers to join your email list, you can more easily build a relationship and promote products — either your products or affiliate products.

To get viewers on your email list, you have to start by asking yourself why someone would want to receive emails from you. While it was cool back in the day to offer a newsletter, no one is in a rush to get more emails in their inboxes. Instead, you have to give them a free incentive to get them on your email list.

I've done a variety of free offers from free eBooks to video series to virtual summit tickets. However, what will work the best for YouTube are video based freebies that are easy to consume.

Video based freebies work for YouTube because YouTube viewers have been conditioned to watch videos. If you give them a free video series and just ask them to enter their name and email address, they're more likely to do it since they already watch videos. Offering a mini training course also works well because viewers can opt-in and then binge on the course later.

But you also have to factor in that people are very busy. The first freebies I offered were eBooks. These did well initially, but as time wore on, people wanted freebies that were easier to consume. As more people offered free eBooks, they all became much harder to read due to the time factor.

That's where checklists come into play, and the great thing about checklists is that they're also very easy to create. While it can take several days to create an entire eBook, it just takes a few minutes to create a checklist. Just create a list of tasks for people to perform and you have your checklist.

Your niche will determine which of these options is the better play, but if you can, I recommend starting off with the checklist just because they are so easy to create.

Once you decide what kind of freebie you will offer, the next step is deciding on the right topic. The first eBook I gave out for free was called <u>27 Ways To Get More Retweets On Twitter</u>. It's still a great resource for people who want exposure on Twitter, but Twitter related content isn't getting as much demand as it was when I first came out with that eBook.

In addition, almost none of the videos I post nowadays are about Twitter, so offering this eBook at the end of each of my videos doesn't make much sense. Now I talk more about YouTube, podcasting, and making money with your content. Checklists for YouTube, podcasting, and content monetization make more sense than a Twitter eBook.

And since checklists are so easy to create, you can create a custom checklist for each core topic you talk about on your channel. That way, you'll have an offer specifically tailored to your video topic which will help your conversion rate.

Creating The Funnel

Once you decide on your freebie, the next step is to make a funnel. Creating a profitable funnel and driving traffic to that funnel is the path from newbie to pro YouTuber. A basic definition of a funnel is a sequence of emails and pages that lead into one another.

Here's an example of a typical funnel I create for one of my virtual summits:

- The landing page asks for a name and email address in exchange for a free ticket to the summit
- When someone subscribes, they get led to an upsell page that invites that person to buy the All-Access Pass to get lifetime access to all of the sessions
- When someone buys the All-Access Pass, they get led to an upsell page that invites them to buy a relevant course based on the summit or join the Advanced Influencer Mastermind

Some people will buy all of your upsells right away, but that won't always be the case. In between each of those actions is a series of emails that warms people up and eventually turns them into buyers of the upsell they didn't buy when they first saw it.

If someone doesn't buy the All-Access Pass, I send an email each day with the sessions coming out for that day. In each of those emails, I tell attendees they can get lifetime access to the summit through the All-Access Pass.

If someone buys an All-Access Pass, I don't want that person in the email sequence that urges people to buy the All-Access Pass. A funnel has different paths. The path an individual takes within your funnel depends on which actions they have and haven't taken.

If a funnel sounds difficult to create, it is something I help people with, and you can reach out to me marc@marcguberti.com to see if we're a good fit. But if you want to create your own funnel, I'm going to give a brief overview.

You only need a few things to create an effective funnel:

#1: An email marketing service provider — ConvertKit, Aweber, and MailChimp are some of the many great options. MailChimp is the best one if you're on a budget and is a viable email marketing service provider in its own right (i.e. just because it's the cheapest doesn't mean it's bad. It's actually pretty good but I personally use ConvertKit).

#2: Software to create opt-in pages and sales pages — ClickFunnels is great for anyone and is super easy to use. If you already have a WordPress.org website, I recommend OptimizePress. LeadPages is also a viable option.

#3: A way to process payments — ClickFunnels and ThriveCart are great options. They also allow you to recruit affiliates to promote your products.

While ClickFunnels is the closest thing to an all-in-one resource and has the most features, it does cost $97/mo at its lowest package while OptimizePress and ThriveCart are both one-off purchases. Again, I can do the funnel for you if you are interested. If not, those are the resources you should focus on when creating your funnel.

Getting Sponsorships
When your channel starts to pick up momentum, you can approach brands with sponsorship proposals. Reaching to brands with sponsorship proposals is a more lucrative way to put ads on your channel than by using Google Adsense.

I wouldn't recommend this approach until you at least have at least 1,000 subscribers and some engagement for your videos. Some channels with smaller audiences but higher engagement can take the sponsorship path sooner.

Regardless of when you start, sponsors will look at your audience size and engagement to determine if sponsoring a video on your channel makes sense for them. Likewise, the larger your audience and the more engagement you have, the higher prices you can charge for sponsorships.

Depending on your niche, the sponsor, and what the sponsorship entails, you can command a rate between $10 and $50 per 1,000 views. If you can get 10,000 views, you could charge anywhere from $100 to $500 for a sponsorship placement (assuming none of the views are bought).

However, you don't need 10,000 views per video to charge sponsors $100 to $500. All you have to do is ensure 10,000 views, and those 10,000 views can come from multiple videos. The same is true for charging $10 to $50 for video(s) that combine to get 1,000 views.

If you are a smaller YouTuber, one way you can make more money from sponsorships is by creating multiple packages where your starter pack is multiple videos. Let's say you average 50 views for each of your videos.

You can offer...
- A $5 package for placement in 4 of your videos (200 views)

- A $10 package for placement in 10 of your videos (500 views)
- A $15 package for placement in 20 of your videos (1,000 views)

These numbers are just examples. You can change the price or the number of videos you include based on your preference, niche, and what the sponsorship entails. As you get more views and engagement for each of your videos, you can raise your prices.

The key to this example is to demonstrate that you're offering packages instead of sponsoring one video for a small price, and you're incentivizing sponsors to commit to bigger packages. If a sponsor buys three of the $5 packages, you get 600 views. However, buying the $15 package upfront gives the same sponsor 1,000 views and additional videos.

Adding a few zeroes in dollar amounts and total views shows how sponsorship revenue can add up when your channel grows…

- A $50 package for placement in 4 of your videos (2K views)
- A $100 package for placement in 10 of your videos (5K views)
- A $150 package for placement in 20 of your videos (10K views)

Understanding this principle now will help you make thousands of extra dollars each month if you grow your audience and gradually raise your prices when approaching sponsors.

Where To Find Sponsors
When you are ready to enter sponsorships, you have to find sponsors and reach out to them. One of the secret ways to find sponsors for your YouTube channel is through Fiverr. I wouldn't rely on Fiverr for this approach, and it probably won't make you a full-

time income, but it's a great way to get discovered without doing much work.

In my experience, if you can get some initial Fiverr sales on your own, you'll get discovered in Fiverr's search engine and sponsors will seek you out instead of the other way around.

You can also mention that you're accepting sponsors for your YouTube channel to your audience, friends, and people in your network.

You can also find sponsors by seeing who is currently sponsoring YouTubers and podcasters. Brands that currently sponsor creators have a better idea of the entire process and would be easier to sell on the idea of sponsoring some of the videos on your channel. In my experience, it's much easier to find who's sponsoring podcast episodes because podcast hosts list the sponsor in the show note links.

Furthermore, while most big podcasters have sponsors on their shows, you don't always see that with YouTubers who already have Adsense and other income streams rolling in.

There are some brands that haven't sponsored YouTubers or pod-casters in the past but would be happy to sponsor you if you can pitch your YouTube channel the right way.

Asking For Donations
While I don't recommend this path for every niche, there are some niches where creators often ask their viewers for donations. This is usually a niche where there's a stronger emphasis on entertainment

than education. The difference is that for educational content, it's easier to create products and services around that content than around entertainment-based content (Note: It is possible to create products and services around entertainment-based content as well depending on how creative you get, but some topics are harder than others. Reach out to me marc@marcguberti.com if you can't come up with a product or service around your topic).

I always recommend looking for a way to offer a product or service as those can be more lucrative, but depending on your niche and audience, asking for donations can also bring in a reliable stream of income.

The popular resource of choice for most YouTubers is Patreon. You can also use something like ThriveCart to make it possible for people to donate to you without going through Patreon's platform.

By using something like ThriveCart to collect payments, you'll keep 100% of the money your viewers donate to you each month, and it won't be as confusing as Patreon. I briefly made a push for Patreon to get donations for my YouTube channel, and multiple people told me they had a problem with using Patreon's site and becoming patrons.

If you do ask for donations, give people an incentive to donate. If you are in the educational sphere, give your donors exclusive content each week or month depending on what makes the most sense for your channel and your audience's expectations. If you are in the entertainment sphere, shout outs are one of the many incentives you can offer to get donations.

Part 4

Video Marketing

We've covered how to create great videos and set them up so they make money. Now we will talk about promoting those videos so they reach your ideal audience and nurture your existing community.

The more effectively you promote your videos, the more people you'll reach. This will set you up to make more revenue from your videos.

Effective video marketing starts with becoming fully aware of all of your current marketing assets. Many people have a variety of social media handles that they rarely use. These are the places to start when marketing your videos because they are the low hanging fruits

That way, not only do you promote your videos and grow on YouTube, but you'll also grow on other social networks in the process. Earlier I talked about how I write LinkedIn Articles around my videos. Not only does this strategy help me grow on YouTube, but it also helps me get more LinkedIn connections who may turn into clients in the future.

My belief is that, with the exception of video-focused social networks, posting once a day on each social network is very doable. For Twitter, you just send out a brief tweet. For Instagram, you find a photo in your library and post it. If you don't have a photo readily available, you can easily create a photo using something like Canva. Same thing for Facebook and most of the other social networks.

We'll talk about different marketing assets so you have a better picture of which ones to use and how you can get more exposure for your videos and channel.

What To Do On Each Social Network

Social media has been around long enough for many of us to create accounts on these platforms and know that they can help you grow your business. Rather than do a complete rundown on each of these social networks and their strengths, I'm going to share how you can use a few key social networks to spread awareness for your YouTube videos and channel.

You'll notice some of these tactics are repetitive while others are specifically for that social network. The deeper you go into social media marketing, the more you'll realize they are all the same.

Instagram
- Post a picture of you editing or a picture of your thumbnail and tell your audience that you're working on your next video
- Share that same post in your Instagram story
- Create a few Instagram stories that tell your followers what they'll learn from the video and when it's going to drop

- If you have the swipe up feature, give that option to people who want to see your video
- Take clips of the video and post it on IG TV and your Instagram feed
- Do an IG Live to promote your upcoming video
- Change the link in your bio to your YouTube Channel Page

Facebook
- Post a picture of you editing or a picture of your thumbnail and tell your audience that you're working on your next video. You can also do this with text since pictures aren't required to post on Facebook
- Share that same post in your Facebook story
- Create a few Facebook stories that tell your followers what they'll learn from the video and when it's going to drop
- Participate in Facebook Groups. Make sure your header promotes your YouTube channel. That's how you get members from Facebook Groups to check out your YouTube channel
- Take clips of the video and post it on Facebook Watch
- Do a Facebook Live to promote your upcoming video

LinkedIn
- Post a picture of you editing or a picture of your thumbnail and tell your audience that you're working on your next video. You can also do this with text since pictures aren't required to post on LinkedIn
- Participate in LinkedIn Groups. Make sure your header promotes your YouTube channel. That's how you get members from LinkedIn Groups to check out your YouTube channel
- Share clips of the video and post it to LinkedIn
- Do a LinkedIn Live to promote your upcoming video

- Create LinkedIn Articles around each of your videos and core video topics

Twitter
- Post a picture of you editing or a picture of your thumbnail and tell your audience that you're working on your next video. You can also do this with text since pictures aren't required to post on Twitter
- Share clips of the video and post it to Twitter
- Do a Twitter Live (Periscope) to promote your upcoming video

SnapChat
- Post a picture of you editing or a picture of your thumbnail and tell your audience that you're working on your next video.
- Share clips of the video and post them to your SnapChat story

Pinterest
- Post a picture of you editing or a picture of your thumbnail and tell your audience that you're working on your next video.
- Share clips of the video and post it on Pinterest

Many of the tactics are all the same. Rather than wrap all of these tasks under one umbrella and say, "Do this for each social network," I decided to share them this way to give you a better understanding of the work that's involved.

The more of these you can check off with each video, the closer you'll get to maximizing your social media marketing assets. One of the big mistakes people make is focusing on growing their audiences to the point where they forget about engaging with their existing audience and providing that better experience.

Creating teaser content and providing unique value to each social network you're on will give people a reason to follow you on all of the social networks instead of just on their favorite 1-2 platforms.

The idea is that regardless of which platform someone's using, that person sees one of your videos or is informed about one of your upcoming videos. Social media does an incredible job at grabbing people's attention. The only way to grab people's attention with social media on a large scale is by doing a little bit on each one.

Even though it's good to play favorites and focus on your top social networks in the beginning, it's good to be a little active on each one. Just make sure you are more active on the social networks that give you the best results.

Strategic Outreach

Social media marketing's sole purpose is to put your content in front of more people. In fact, that's the purpose of marketing as a whole. You want more people to see your videos…you promote them.

Success in business at its very core is getting to know people who eventually get to know, like, and trust you. It's all about relationship building and being in the right circles. When you create content, you have the opportunity to impact people. Some people in your audience will find you through YouTube's discoverability options (i.e. suggested videos, search engine traffic, etc.).

However, you can and should always connect with people on a 1-to-1 level regardless of how much your channel grows.

One of my favorite ways of connecting with people on a 1-to-1 level is LinkedIn. I'll send at least 20 connection requests per day and engage with the people who connect with me. Some of the people I engage with on LinkedIn turn into clients. If someone doesn't want to become a client but wants to still learn about podcasting, YouTube, social media marketing, or something similar, I tell that person about my YouTube channel.

This tactic may get you a few subscribers each day, but they're subscribers who you know and can keep track of. You can see what these individuals are posting to their social networks and ask if they have any questions related to your niche. This can inspire future content ideas and boost your revenue. If you have a few hundred subscribers who know you very well, and you combine that with an irresistible offer, it's not farfetched for you to make $1000s each month from your YouTube channel. Just keep coming out with great videos, engaging with your audience, and some people in that audience will become customers.

1-to-1 relationship building takes more work than sending out a tweet or publishing a new video that instantly reaches your followers. However, you're not the only game in town. The people following you on Twitter and subscribing to your YouTube channel are also paying attention to other creators. Just because someone's subscribed to your channel doesn't guarantee that person will watch each of your new videos.

For some people, keeping their attention will involve 1-to-1 relationship building. Determine who your core fans are and reach out to them each time you come out with a new video. These core fans

are very likely to view the video and share it with their friends…
especially if you treat them like core fans.

My inbox is always crowded with emails. I scroll through most of
the emails in my inbox, but I pay attention and even read the
emails from the people who I have a deeper relationship with.

For instance, one person who I pay closer attention to than the average person in my inbox is Daymond John. I was an ambassador
for two of his books, met him at a book signing for one of his
books, and he called my cell number and had a two minute conversation with me.

In the grand scheme of things, building that 1-on-1 relationship
wasn't incredibly time consuming. We had a two minute conversation where it was just us, he gave me and the other ambassadors a
shoutout at his NYC book signing event, I got to give him a hand-
shake and get my copy signed, and he sent ambassadors nice swag
related to his book.

But that time investment is the reason I pay attention to Daymond's email in the cluster of emails that show up in my inbox.

Getting on 5-10 minute calls with your fans is such an underrated
way to grow your YouTube channel. Messaging people and devel-
oping the 1-to-1 relationships is also very underrated. People just
want to click a button and put their message in front of thousands
of people because it's easier and sounds more impressive than
building 1-to-1 relationships.

Some YouTubers have that leverage. Some people can even get in front of millions of people with the click of a button. However, no one started that way, and it's these deeper relationships that will get you there.

Even someone like Daymond who not only can get in front of millions of people with the click of a button but is also on *Shark Tank* values the deeper relationships and invests in 1-to-1 phone calls.

This is the power of strategic outreach, and it's the one leverage point smaller YouTubers have on the bigger guys and gals. People like Daymond can't reach out to every single person in their audiences on a 1-to-1 level. However, smaller YouTubers have fewer people in their audiences which makes it easier for them to develop the 1-to-1 relationships that turn causal viewers into super fans.

If I only had 10 subscribers on my YouTube channel, I'd be jumping on quick calls with all 10 of those subscribers. I'd ask them what kind of content they'd like to see on the channel and what they're currently working on. Personalized messages on places like LinkedIn work wonders as well, but nothing gets close to the phone call and face-to-face interactions.

When you reach out to fans and turn them into super fans, they're more likely to promote your channel and brand to their friends. However, you have to tap beyond your super fans as well. You have to build new relationships with people who currently don't know who you are.

So how do we get strategic with our outreach? How do we reach out to the right people who are more inclined to subscribe to our channels and share your content?

Here are a few places to look for ideal people who don't know who you are...

- **Engage with other people's retweeters.** Find a successful creator in your space who gets a bunch of retweets for each thing they share. For me, I like to go to Lewis Howes' and Gary Vaynerchuk's Twitter accounts and see who's retweeting their content. Then, I reach out to each person who retweeted the tweet and start a conversation with that person. If that person responds, I put that person's username in a spreadsheet. I then know to occasionally reach out to these people (weekly or monthly depending on the relationship).

- **Search for desirable traits, roles, characteristics, etc**. If you want to reach out to authors, search for the keyword author and filter it to only show people's profiles. That way, you'll only see the people on that social network who are also authors. You can use this same approach to follow a specific hashtag. Engage with those people, and put the usernames of people who responds into the spreadsheet.

- **Go to in-person events and network with people**. We live in an increasingly digital world that, no matter how digital it becomes, will still be filled with people. Talking to people behind a computer screen is more scalable, but when you attend events and talk to people, you can quickly turn people who know nothing about you into super fans. Under ideal circumstances, you're the speaker at that event (something we talk about on the Profitable Public Speaking Podcast). However, you can also reap plenty of benefits as an attendee who networks with people throughout the day. A bonus tip if you're in this spot is to organize a Meet-Up if you can just before the event, after one of the event days, or after the entire event to get in a speaking gig and do more networking.

- **Participate in social media groups**. I briefly mentioned Facebook and LinkedIn Groups before. These are both great ways to network with communities that are interested in the type of content you post on your channel. However, don't spam these groups with links to your newest videos. Instead, build relationships and answer people's questions. If your header demonstrates to people that you have a YouTube channel and urges them to subscribe, more people in those groups will become YouTube subscribers. Reddit is one of the harder social networks to master, and it's not included in this book. If you do self-promotion on Reddit the wrong way, let's just say you won't have an enjoyable experience on Reddit. However, if you can master that social network and engage in the right groups, you can get a gigantic surge in views and subscribers.

- **Start a podcast and interview people**. One of the strategies I teach my podcasting clients is how they can turn some of their guests into clients and super fans. I release three interview-based episodes across my podcasts each week and may raise that number in the future (this doesn't include the number of people who I interview for my evergreen virtual summits). During each interview, you can mention your YouTube channel and/or your product or service. During the post-conversation, some of your guests will have questions and may subscribe to your channel or buy your product or service. Not to mention most of these guests will then promote the episode to their communities and attract more people to your brand that way as well.

Reaching out to people is key to becoming successful in any niche. Making outreach a foundational piece of your YouTube strategy will pay great dividends as you build new relationships each day.

Collaborate With Other YouTubers

One of the big themes I like to hit on is that you can only do so much marketing on your own. To expand your potential, you have to get more people to help you with marketing your content. This is one of the reasons I interview people on my podcast. They'll promote the episode when it goes live which will help me reach more people. This is a win-win relationship since I also promote each episode to my audience.

Collaborations on YouTube is similar in some ways and different in others. From an interviewing standpoint, it's ideal for the video if you and the interviewee are in the same room. If you can't meet your guest and do the interview live, I like to focus in on one part of a podcast interview and turn that part into a standalone video. This is what I did when Jess Tiffany came on the Profitable Public Speaking Podcast.

As a side note, when you are at events and want to interview some people there, don't wait until after the event to schedule an interview. Try to interview some of them at the event for 5-10 minutes. It's a more engaging video when you're both in the same room.

But going back to collaborating with other YouTubers, there are a variety of ways you can create the actual content. Interviewing a YouTuber, taking turns sharing best tips around a certain topic, or playing a video game together (more for gaming channels, but I've seen business channels do this a little bit) are some of the ways you can collaborate. You might have more options depending on your niche, but those are some ways to start.

Coming up with the creative ideas and producing the content are the easy parts. You either record together or do your parts separately. The hard part is finding other YouTubers to collaborate with. It's even more difficult to find YouTubers who will collaborate with you over the long-term.

Once the initial collaboration is successful, you can start to think long-term with that creator. However, finding people to collaborate with is the first step. While there are a few websites and other tools that focus on helping you find YouTubers to collaborate with, in my experience, many of those didn't work well.

I found more success with arranging collaborations when I found YouTubers in my niche with similarly sized audiences as me. You want to find YouTubers with audiences close to your size so it's possible for you both to mutually benefit from the collaboration.

I started by searching for keywords in my niche and filter the results by channel. However, when you search a phrase like "social media marketing" and filter by channel, you're primarily going to get the channels with "social media marketing" in their name. I've found some potential collaborators through this method who are now in dialogue with me, but it's not the best method.

The best strategy is to start by growing your channel and get sub-scribers. You'll have to do this anyway to lock in collaborations with YouTubers who have big audiences. But that's not where the magic happens.

Once you have some subscribers on your channel, I want you to go through each of those subscribers and see what channels they are subscribed to. This is very hit-or-miss, but if you look through enough of your subscribers, you'll find some great YouTubers you can collaborate with.

Here's why this is very hit-or-miss...

• Some of your subscribers won't let you see who they are sub-scribed to. This is an option YouTube gives each user, and if you can't see who a subscriber is subscribed to, it's impossible to proceed with this strategy for that subscriber

• Some of your subscribers will publicize who they are subscribed to. However, on closer look, it's only the bigger YouTube chan-nels that you don't have much of a chance to collaborate with. As I write this book, I'm at around 3,600 subscribers. Some of the channels my subscribers are also subscribed to are Grant Cardone and Gary Vaynerchuk. Both of those entrepreneurs are very influential and have millions of YouTube subscribers. Re-member, our focus is on mutually beneficial relationships from an audience growth standpoint. If I were to ask Grant or Gary to collaborate, it's pretty clear who benefits much more from the collaboration, especially if it's a long-term one.

- Some of your subscribers who publicize who they are subscribed to will be subscribed to a variety of smaller channels
  which only a few hundred or thousand subscribers apiece. This
  is where you hit the jackpot. You'll come across YouTubers you
  probably haven't heard of before but who consistently create
  new content and get engagement for their videos. Find some of
  those people who have an audience size close to yours, and start
  reaching out.

The more subscribers you have on your channel, the more likely
you'll find great channels for collaborations. I go through all of the
subscribers YouTube lets me see to discover not only who I can
collaborate with, but also what additional channels my viewers are
watching. Knowing many of my subscribers are also subscribed to
Grant Cardone and Gary Vaynerchuk gives me an idea of what
content I should create for my audience in the future.

And the great thing about collaborations is that as you do more of
them, more people will reach out to you and ask if they can do collaborations with you. One of the not-so-hidden secrets to collaborations is that you're not the only one in your niche looking for
them. If you make it clear that you do collaborations, and you publish collaboration videos, more of your viewers will reach out and
ask to do a collaboration with you.

Requests from other people can also be very hit-or-miss as some
collaboration requests won't be mutually beneficial, but it will feel
good to get collaboration requests instead of searching for channels for collaboration purposes.

Push Out Micro Content And Treat Each Video Like A Launch
Micro content are the smaller pieces of content that are related to
the longer videos you put out. You can upload parts of your videos
to other social networks to drive more buzz for your upcoming
YouTube videos.

I prefer to upload teaser videos to my other social networks to lead
up to the release of my YouTube videos. Treat each of your videos
like a mini product launch. Reach out to people in your network
and see if they could share the video with their audiences. Build up
anticipation for your videos and offer an incentive for people who
watch the video and subscribe to your channel.

If you have a digital product or coupon, you could offer one person who leaves a comment free access to your digital product or a
coupon for a future order. That way, you'll drive more engagement
for your videos and get the YouTube algorithm to push your content.

**Use The Community Tab To Engage With Your Current You-
Tube Audience**
Much of the marketing has been focused on what to do outside of
YouTube. However, there are ways to market your videos within
YouTube. One of the best ways to promote your videos within
YouTube is to use the Community Tab to engage with your sub-
scribers.

You can write a new post telling your subscribers what video
you're currently working on and what they can soon expect on
your channel. The Community Tab is also a great way to engage
with your subscribers and get their attention. That way, instead of

just working your way towards a big number of subscribers, the Community Tab combined with quality content will allow you to work your way to way to a big number of engaged subscribers.

Here are some ideas of what to post on YouTube within the community tab:

- What video you're currently working on
- When a new video or live stream is set to come out
- Promote a product or service
- Inspiration or motivation depending on which word you prefer to use
- Share a blog post, podcast episode, or one of your other social networks — bounce your subscribers around
- Your collaborators' channels. Usually, that collaborator will share your channel in their Community Tab
- Any good news about your business (i.e. getting a new sponsor, getting new clients, etc.)

It's good to post something new in the YouTube Community Tab several times per week. The more often you use the Community Tab, the more your audience will notice you and remember your channel in the sea of other options.

The Community Tab can also be a great way to bounce people around to your other places. This is especially important for growing your social media presence. Here's an example of how this works...

Let's say you post one of your Instagram pictures in the YouTube Community Tab and urge your subscribers to follow you on Instagram. Some of those people will follow you on Instagram and engage with your Instagram content.

That's going to help you in the Instagram algorithm…and if you use Instagram to promote your YouTube channel, then that's also going to help you in YouTube's algorithm. We've covered having your other social networks point to your YouTube channel, but you can also use the YouTube Community Tab and your videos to point to your other social networks.

Right now, I primarily focus on promoting Instagram on my YouTube channel due to the sizes of my social media platforms. I am at around 470,000 Twitter followers and 47,000 Pinterest followers. On Instagram, I'm at a little over 5,000 followers. That's my social media account that needs the most help from an audience size perspective. Cross promoting YouTube and Instagram allows me to expand my reach on both of those platforms.

You can focus on a social network other than Instagram or cross promote multiple social networks. However, there is a point in there where you have to focus on promoting your upcoming video and the product or service that will actually make you money.

That's why I focus on Instagram instead of also promoting the other social networks. Too much social media cross promotion doesn't give you an opportunity to turn your YouTube subscribers into email subscribers.

Create A Live Video Series
YouTube started allowing their users to go live on their platform well before most of the other social networks did. YouTube Live is

one of the top features on YouTube for growing your audience, getting essential watch time for becoming a YouTube Partner, and making money with your content.

The most effective YouTube Live series work like TV shows. You have a set day of the week and a set time. As you do YouTube Lives more consistently, your subscribers will know that you'll be live at the same time and day of week.

Live videos are more engaging than regular videos because viewers feel closer to the creator. It's not a replay. It's the real deal, and your viewers will have the ability to post their questions and other thoughts in real time knowing that the person going live will see those comments.

In live video series, it's essential for you to interact with your fans. This will create a stronger bond between you and your audience, and it will be the reason that people come back for more of your live videos.

Before you go live, make sure you do enough preparation so you can talk about your topic for at least 30-60 minutes. The longer you can talk during your live video, the better. I've seen some live video creators do lives that have stretched on for many hours. According to Ad Week, the longest YouTube Live ever recorded was an astounding 571 hours.

While I don't recommend that length of time for anyone, if you can talk for a few hours instead of the usual 30-60 minutes in an engaging way, go for it. Your watch time (and therefore the YouTube algorithm) will thank you.

When it comes to promoting and making money from the YouTube Live, you have to treat it like an educational webinar. You should inform your audience about the Live at the following times...

- 3 days before your YouTube Live
- 2 days before your YouTube Live
- 1 day before your YouTube Live
- 1 hour before your YouTube Live
- 5 minutes before your YouTube Live

These times are just like a webinar launch. You'll drive more attention and engagement to your channel and likely see a surge in subscribers if you fully implement the marketing plan.

YouTube has a built-in feature for conducting Live videos, but third party apps are also a great option. As of writing, YouTube's built-in feature doesn't let you share your screen or slides, so the third party apps will be the better option for most people right now. Ecamm Live, Zoom, Crowdcast, and OBS Studio are some options to consider for conducting YouTube Lives via 3rd party apps.

Part 5

Video Optimization

Video optimization does take extra time, but it's well worth it. For my initial videos, I didn't care much about optimizing my content to perform on YouTube's search engine. I wrote a basic description just to get it done. I chose one of the three thumbnails YouTube gives you. I didn't bother adding things like cards and end-screens that are meant to get more engagement and subscribers for your channel.

Ideally, you should optimize your videos before you publish them. However, this is a step that many YouTubers ignore because creating the content feels like the achievement.

Don't get me wrong, it's an achievement to create content…but that content isn't doing any good if it's not getting seen by enough people. You could promote it with the strategies and tactics we discussed earlier, but by not optimizing your content, you're sabotaging your video from getting more exposure on YouTube's search engine.

Optimizing your YouTube videos allows YouTube to know what your videos are about. If YouTube can't tell what your videos are about, they won't promote your videos in the right places which will hurt your exposure.

All matured, successful channels get the majority of their traffic from YouTube's search engine. You'll still have to drive your own traffic to their videos, but you know you have a successful You-Tube channel when most of the traffic you get is from YouTube's search engine and suggested videos.

If those are your main traffic streams, you can expect your channel to quickly pick up momentum.

Keyword Research
I briefly covered this topic already, but this is the first step to video optimization. Doing keyword research before you create the actual content allows you to create content on ideas that have a higher likelihood of performing well.

For instance, I was originally going to create a bunch of videos around virtual summits. However, this is a very niche topic that didn't have enough traction going for it in that moment on You-Tube.

I decided to focus on topics that were already in demand on You-Tube such as podcasting and content marketing.

Virtual summits are a hot topic and more people want to launch them, but that topic haven't really taken off on YouTube. Neither demand nor supply are there. I'm all down for creating content around an area of expertise where there's little supply, but if that low supply is accompanied by low demand, there isn't a point to creating that content. As soon as the demand is there, I'll ramp up on virtual summit videos to account for the lack of supply

There are many great options available, so wasting time on a topic that doesn't have much demand will make it harder for you to grow your YouTube channel.

vidIQ and Tube Buddy are the two YouTube keyword tool choices for me. The former makes it easy to find out how well certain keywords are performing and the latter makes it easier to come up with a string of tags for your videos.

When you find the right keywords, it's important to use them often in your description and towards the front of your title.

In one of my videos "How To Get More Youtube Views On A Video In The First 24 Hours | YouTube Marketing," I took a few keywords and incorporated them within the title and description of the video.

Here are some of the many keywords I optimized the video for:
- How To Get More YouTube Views On A Video In The First 24 Hours
- YouTube Marketing
- YouTube SEO
- How To Rank Your YouTube Videos

Two of those keywords are in the title:
How To Get More Youtube Views On A Video In The First 24 Hours | YouTube Marketing

And I've used bold font to show the keywords as they appear in the description.

> Discover **how to get more views on YouTube fast within the first 24 hours** of your video getting published. These tips will help you rank your videos higher and achieve massive YouTube growth.

> You'll also learn about **YouTube SEO** for the long-term, **how to rank your YouTube videos**, and of course, **how to get more YouTube views on a video in the first 24 hours**.

Instead of listing one keyword after the other in the description, I include the keywords in a readable format for the viewer. This is how you write for the person and the search engine.

Upload Defaults

The description I shared earlier is just a small excerpt of what one of my video descriptions looks like. All of my descriptions are at least 2,000 characters, and I have plans to extend that character count.

The reason I can easily write 2,000+ character descriptions is because I fill up the default description that shows up for all of my videos. At least 80% of the descriptions of all of my recently uploaded videos are exactly the same.

I previously copied and pasted the default description I wanted in each of my videos. However, the default description is a much better option that streamlines the process. You can find this option in your settings and create the default description for all future uploads. The default description is a great starter point, but it should never be the actual description.

In the default description, I tell viewers how they can subscribe, promote some of my business resources (with affiliate links), the link they can use to schedule a free strategy call with me, some of my freebies, and a bio for my and my channel.

It's a lot of calls-to-action, so make sure you put your most important CTAs near the top of your description. Asking people to subscribe to your YouTube channel or watch your other videos should be the first call-to-action. This is how you keep people's attention on YouTube and elsewhere for a longer period of time instead of getting their attention once and then not getting it again for a long time.

Creating Great Thumbnails For Your Videos

Your thumbnail is one of the key factors that determines how many people will clickthrough and watch your video. A good thumbnail and a bad thumbnail is the difference between dominating the YouTube algorithm and getting zero momentum.

Too many people make the mistake of not taking thumbnails seriously and choosing one of the three options YouTube gives you. The thumbnail options YouTube gives you are not optimized to perform well on their search engine.

Interestingly, you may notice that none of the YouTube thumbnails you see on top of the search results are one of the three default options YouTube gives you.

Thumbnails need the right combination of background, people, pictures and text to thrive in the YouTube ecosystem.

My advice for creating thumbnails is to look at other great thumbnails with the same keyword and see what elements they are using. Pay attention to the color of text, what logos are getting used, and how other YouTubers include pictures of themselves in their thumbnail.

Most of the effective thumbnails have under 5 words, a picture of the YouTuber, and at least one other picture. What you'll find depends on your niche, but there is one thing to avoid. Make sure you avoid putting any text, logos, or other important details on the bottom right of the thumbnail.

Because of the way YouTube works, these parts won't be as visible to your audience as the middle right or entire left of your thumbnail. The upper right is a little more visible but still not a good place to put important parts of your thumbnail. It's better to put words, logos, and other important stuff on the left side of the thumbnail and a picture of you on the right side of the thumbnail.

To illustrate this example, I included the thumbnail for one of my Instagram videos called "How To Create Consistent Content On Instagram | Instagram Marketing Strategy."

This is the first video of my Instagram series, so it took some time to create this thumbnail. All of the Instagram related videos I post to YouTube will have a similar look so people can tell my Instagram related videos apart from other people's Instagram related videos.

The text is on the left, the big Instagram logo is on the center, and my picture is to the right. The smaller Instagram pictures are spread out across the video thumbnail because a similar strategy has been working well for my YouTube related videos.

However, look at what happens when you're searching for the video on YouTube...

The timestamp and the watch later clock both take up a significant amount of the right portion of the video thumbnail. Luckily, it's just a picture of me. You can look at that thumbnail and still know what the video is about. However, if "Consistent Content" was on the right side of the video, and part of it was covered by 5:47, it would be less clear and therefore hurt my clickthrough rate. The timestamp will take up a higher percentage of space when your video appears in suggested videos.

It's not necessary to see all of the buttons on my shirt to know what the video is about, and no one's clicking on this thumbnail because of my shirt. However, if the Instagram logo or any of the text was covered instead, that would hurt the thumbnail's click-through rate.

Add Cards And End-Screens To Your Videos
The data YouTube gives you is incredible to the point where it's hard to figure out what to do with all of this data.

One piece of data that matters for your channel is your video's retention rate. You can see when people are dropping off, and this can help you create better videos in the future.

However, it can also help you get more traffic to your other videos.

One thing YouTube lets you do is add cards to your videos. These cards will appear on the upper right side of your videos and encourage viewers to do things such as watch another video or go to your website.

One of my videos below has a 36.8% retention rate. At 2:13, the average viewer stops watching and decides to watch another video.

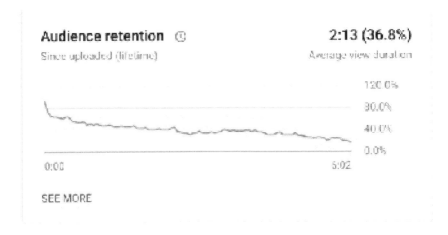

Some viewers may stop watching because they see a good video on the suggested list of videos. Others may just decide to go back to YouTube's homepage.

Regardless of why they stop watching, YouTube's data shows 2:13 is the mark. A 36.8% retention rate isn't bad. It's not spectacular, but not bad.

It's good to watch the video to try and figure out why people are leaving at that mark. In fact, you should also rewatch your videos on the parts where you can see a big drop in the video's retention rate within a short stretch. However, you can also do something with the video.

While you can't re-upload a new file and entirely change the video, you can add cards throughout your video. At the 2-minute mark, I added a card that recommends a related video on my channel.

It's important to add this card just before the 2:13 mark because people don't just decide to leave at the 2:13 mark. It's 15 seconds before when the person starts to consider leaving and then at 2:13, people leave.

If you present another option at the 2-minute mark (or your equivalent based on what your data tells you), you'll get more people to view more of your videos instead of someone clicking on a suggested video and possibly not viewing any of your videos for the rest of their session on YouTube.

I now added this card to my YouTube video that shows another video about how you can get your first 100,000 views on YouTube.

Normally I'd change the thumbnail because the 100,000 views part is covered by the 12:20 timestamp, but I'm only keeping it the way it is because the thumbnail has a solid clickthrough rate.

Regardless, instead of someone leaving at the 2:13 mark, they might leave slightly earlier, but I am able to move my viewers around from video to video across my channel. A few days after publishing a video, I will go into the analytics, check the retention rate, and add a card like this to send people to another video.

Some people do watch the video all the way to the end. The analytics show this to be true. However, providing this option at the two minute mark will allow you to keep more of the viewers who are thinking of tuning out.

People who are enjoying your current video and also like the video from your YouTube Card will also spend more time on your channel. Furthermore, if you spread out these YouTube Cards, you're demonstrating to your new viewers that you produce a ton of valuable content on your channel. That's a good reason for anyone to subscribe.

Add End-Screens To Your Videos

Another important feature for your videos are end-screens. Most people make the mistake of concluding their video in the tradition-al route...and I did this for a while. If you've watched a video where I said something like, "That's all for this video. I hope you enjoyed it...and what I want you to do is dream big, achieve greatness, and unlock your potential...TODAY!" then you've seen this in action.

When you end your videos like this, your viewers will know you are ending and have no reason to stick around.

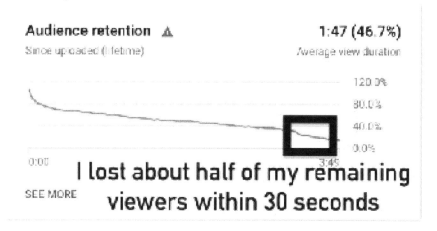

In this video, I lose half of my remaining viewers within 30 sec-onds because I'm doing the traditional video close. Viewers know I'm ending, and who wants to listen to the 1 minute version of, "This video is over"?

Now I abruptly end the video and lead into a short 10-15 second end-screen with music playing in the background.

The abrupt ending gets viewers to the end-screen sooner. This serves as a more valuable ending to the video because it's filled with action steps. If someone clicks on my picture, they have the option to subscribe to my channel.

Those two videos are clickable which gives viewers the opportunity to watch more of my videos. This will help me with the You-Tube algorithm.

I added the "Schedule a free strategy call," "Thanks for watching," and the blue background with my video editing software (Screen-Flow is what I use...but every good video editing software should let you do something this basic).

Similarly to how we discussed bouncing people from social network to social network, you should also bounce viewers from video to video. This end-screen combined with the cards makes that goal easier to achieve.

Create Playlists For Your Channel

One great way to optimize the experience for your viewers and get more traction is through playlists. You can take multiple videos around a similar topic and put those videos in a playlist. This will make it easier for your viewers to binge through specific categories within your channel.

For instance, I have a playlist called "Podcast Monetization + Marketing" which has a bunch of podcasting videos where I teach people how to launch, grow, and monetize their podcasts. Instead of scrolling through my channel to find podcasting related videos, viewers can go through that playlist to find all of my podcasting related videos.

That is the kind of experience you want to create for your viewers. The playlists make it easier for people to browse through your channel the way they want to browse through your channel.

It's very notable that YouTube said a great playlist keep viewers watching longer which will have a positive impact on your watch time, your playlist's ranking, and the rankings of the individual videos.

That's right…playlists also help you with the YouTube algorithm.

Few people know that you can optimize a YouTube playlist so it ranks in YouTube's search engine. When you click on your playlist's link, you'll see the option to edit your playlist.

When you click on edit, you'll have the ability to add a description. By writing a great description for your playlist and filling it with keywords in the process, you can rank your playlist on YouTube's algorithm.

Other editing options you have for your YouTube playlist include the following...

- **Choosing which video's thumbnail is the main thumbnail for your playlist** — pick the thumbnail that has the highest clickthrough rate. You can check the clickthrough rate of each individual video and then choose the winner.
- **Adding and removing videos from the playlist** — I recommend removing videos that aren't doing well and adding a few that make sense and perform well. You don't want to add too many videos to your playlist because viewers would quickly get overwhelmed and not watch your playlist.
- **Ordering the videos on your playlist** — put your highest performing videos on the top of your playlist. "Highest" perform-

ing videos are the ones that have a solid retention rate, get the most subscribers for your channel, the most clicks to your opt-in page, or a combination of the three. It depends on how you measure performance

- **Automatically adding videos to the playlist based on a certain criteria** — I do not recommend this option and believe you should manually add videos to the playlists they should be on when you're about to schedule a video. However, this is an option YouTube provides.

Re-Optimizing Your Older Videos

Many YouTubers are in a rush to create and optimize their new content that they forget about their old content. Some of this content can perform very well if properly re-optimized. When it comes to re-optimizing, the only thing you cannot do is change the video file, but everything else (description, thumbnail, playlist, etc.) can be changed.

Some videos should get more optimization than others. The way you preference your videos is through their retention rate and views.

If a video gets very little views and has a low retention rate, I would ignore it. The videos you should optimize are the ones getting a lot of views and/or have a high retention rate.

For videos with high retention rates, you can get the views by optimizing the description with the keywords you want to rank for and change your video's thumbnail. Then promote the video again and you should start to pick up traffic.

For videos with a lot of views but low retention rates, there's still hope. While you can't upload a new video that reflects what you've learned in this book, you can include a card right before the point where people normally drop off.

Retention rate is something you can't do much about once the video is published, but you can influence what video your viewers watch next. Get some of that traffic from a popular but low retention rate video to your newer videos on similar topics that have the higher retention rates.

Re-optimizing older videos gives you more content to share with your audience. Some YouTubers think they have to come out with a new video each day, but if you re-optimize older videos, you'll save time on the creation process and actually have a library of videos that rank well on YouTube.

Conclusion

YouTube is a platform that will reward creators who keep people on YouTube for a long period of time. The more minutes watched and the higher the clickthrough rate, the more likely you are to thrive on YouTube.

Any creator can make it on YouTube, even if they just start now. While going from 0 to 100,000 subscribers in one year is the exception rather than the rule, the exceptions demonstrate that it's possible even today to build a successful YouTube channel.

Over saturation is just an excuse. Don't use that excuse, keep working on your channel and creating great content, and the results will follow.

If you want to work with me to launch, grow, and monetize your YouTube channel, podcast, or some of your other content, feel free to schedule a free strategy call to see if we're a good fit.

Here's the link to schedule a free strategy call if you are interested: marcguberti.com/strategy

I greatly appreciate you taking the time to read *YouTube Decoded* and hope you enjoy the worksheets. If you enjoyed this book, I would greatly appreciate if you could leave a quick review for this book on Amazon.

Video Creation Worksheet (1)

Video Topic:

_____

Keywords to target for the video:

_____
_____

Key points for the video:

_____
_____
_____
_____

What to mention in the video (i.e. coaching call, training course, opt-in, podcast episode, your next video etc.)

_____
_____

Video Marketing Worksheet (1)

Platforms where you will promote the video (**Suggestions**: Instagram, Facebook, Stories on both of those platforms, Twitter, Pinterest, YouTube Community Tab, LinkedIn, Medium, Blog, Podcast, Email List, etc. — Do what you can handle and then build up):

_____

_____

_____

_____

People you will notify when the video gets published

_____

_____

_____

_____

How you will repurpose your video after its publication

_____

_____

_____

_____

Video Creation Worksheet (2)

Video Topic:

_____

Keywords to target for the video:

_____

_____

Key points for the video:

_____

_____

_____

_____

What to mention in the video (i.e. coaching call, training course, opt-in, podcast episode, your next video etc.)

_____

_____

Video Marketing Worksheet (2)

Platforms where you will promote the video (**Suggestions**: Instagram, Facebook, Stories on both of those platforms, Twitter, Pinterest, YouTube Community Tab, LinkedIn, Medium, Blog, Podcast, Email List, etc. — Do what you can handle and then build up):

_____

_____

_____

_____

People you will notify when the video gets published

_____

_____

_____

_____

How you will repurpose your video after its publication

_____

_____

_____

_____

Video Creation Worksheet (3)

Video Topic:

_____

Keywords to target for the video:

_____

_____

Key points for the video:

_____

_____

_____

_____

What to mention in the video (i.e. coaching call, training course, opt-in, podcast episode, your next video etc.)

_____

_____

Video Marketing Worksheet (3)

Platforms where you will promote the video (**Suggestions**: Instagram, Facebook, Stories on both of those platforms, Twitter, Pinterest, YouTube Community Tab, LinkedIn, Medium, Blog, Podcast, Email List, etc. — Do what you can handle and then build up):

_____

_____

_____

_____

People you will notify when the video gets published

_____

_____

_____

_____

How you will repurpose your video after its publication

_____

_____

_____

_____

Video Creation Worksheet (4)

Video Topic:

_____

Keywords to target for the video:

_____

_____

Key points for the video:

_____

_____

_____

_____

What to mention in the video (i.e. coaching call, training course, opt-in, podcast episode, your next video etc.)

_____

_____

Video Marketing Worksheet (4)

Platforms where you will promote the video (**Suggestions**: Instagram, Facebook, Stories on both of those platforms, Twitter, Pinterest, YouTube Community Tab, LinkedIn, Medium, Blog, Podcast, Email List, etc. — Do what you can handle and then build up):

_____

_____

_____

_____

People you will notify when the video gets published

_____

_____

_____

_____

How you will repurpose your video after its publication

_____

_____

_____

_____

Video Creation Worksheet (5)

Video Topic:

_____

Keywords to target for the video:

_____
_____

Key points for the video:

_____
_____
_____
_____

What to mention in the video (i.e. coaching call, training course, opt-in, podcast episode, your next video etc.)

_____
_____

Video Marketing Worksheet (5)

Platforms where you will promote the video (**Suggestions**: Instagram, Facebook, Stories on both of those platforms, Twitter, Pinterest, YouTube Community Tab, LinkedIn, Medium, Blog, Podcast, Email List, etc. — Do what you can handle and then build up):

_____

_____

_____

_____

People you will notify when the video gets published

_____

_____

_____

_____

How you will repurpose your video after its publication

_____

_____

_____

_____

Video Creation Worksheet (6)

Video Topic:

_____

Keywords to target for the video:

_____

_____

Key points for the video:

_____

_____

_____

_____

What to mention in the video (i.e. coaching call, training course, opt-in, podcast episode, your next video etc.)

_____

_____

Video Marketing Worksheet (6)

Platforms where you will promote the video (**Suggestions**: Instagram, Facebook, Stories on both of those platforms, Twitter, Pinterest, YouTube Community Tab, LinkedIn, Medium, Blog, Podcast, Email List, etc. — Do what you can handle and then build up):

_____

_____

_____

_____

People you will notify when the video gets published

_____

_____

_____

_____

How you will repurpose your video after its publication

_____

_____

_____

_____

Video Creation Worksheet (7)

Video Topic:

_____

Keywords to target for the video:

_____

_____

Key points for the video:

_____

_____

_____

_____

What to mention in the video (i.e. coaching call, training course, opt-in, podcast episode, your next video etc.)

_____

_____

Video Marketing Worksheet (7)

Platforms where you will promote the video (**Suggestions**: Instagram, Facebook, Stories on both of those platforms, Twitter, Pinterest, YouTube Community Tab, LinkedIn, Medium, Blog, Podcast, Email List, etc. — Do what you can handle and then build up):

_____

_____

_____

_____

People you will notify when the video gets published

_____

_____

_____

_____

How you will repurpose your video after its publication

_____

_____

_____

_____

Video Creation Worksheet (8)

Video Topic:

_____

Keywords to target for the video:

_____

_____

Key points for the video:

_____

_____

_____

_____

What to mention in the video (i.e. coaching call, training course, opt-in, podcast episode, your next video etc.)

_____

_____

Video Marketing Worksheet (8)

Platforms where you will promote the video (**Suggestions**: Instagram, Facebook, Stories on both of those platforms, Twitter, Pinterest, YouTube Community Tab, LinkedIn, Medium, Blog, Podcast, Email List, etc. — Do what you can handle and then build up):

_____

_____

_____

_____

People you will notify when the video gets published

_____

_____

_____

_____

How you will repurpose your video after its publication

_____

_____

_____

_____

ɔut The Author

ɔerti is a USA Today and WSJ bestselling author with
ʌ0,000 students in over 180 countries enrolled in his online
ʃes. He is the host of the Breakthrough Success Podcast and
ʌdio Show where listeners learn how to achieve their break-
ɾhroughs. He coaches content creators on how they can attract
more traffic to their content and boost revenue.

If you enjoyed this book, make sure you subscribe to my YouTube
channel (just search "Marc Guberti" on YouTube) for videos that
will help you gain more visibility and revenue with the content
you're creating.

Marc's Other Books

Are you looking for your next book? If so, Marc has written over 20 books which can all be found on Amazon. Here's some of what is waiting for you if you search "Marc Guberti" on Amazon...

Content Marketing Secrets

Discover the key secrets for getting massive traffic and revenue

"This book is a getting-it-done guide for going big in small, manageable steps. Marc has put the playbook together for you." --**Andy Crestodina, author of Content Chemistry**

Podcast Domination

Discover the ultimate podcasting strategies that will help you launch, grow, and monetize your show

"Thorough coverage of the subject. Many books in the topic seem to be teasers to sell premium content. This book is not like that - he covers all topics."
— **Amazon Review**

The Wealthy Author

Discover how to use books to grow your brand and earn passive income.

"If you want to learn more about making more with your books, this is the book you need!" — **Michelle Kulp, best-selling author**

Made in the USA
Middletown, DE
18 November 2019

78949108R00061